# The People
# &
# War

By

Champion Muthle

# DEDICATION

For Bolivar, Pancho Villa, Che, Chiapas, the ANC,
the EFF, the PRC, the PRI, and all guerrillas
everywhere.

# ACKNOWLEDGMENTS

To my grandfathers, Ambition and Charles, my ancestors, and the undying Spirit of the People.

"There's something happening here
What it is ain't exactly clear
There's a man with a gun over there
Telling me I got to beware

I think it's time we stop, children, what's that sound
Everybody look what's going down"

- Buffalo Springfield (1966) *For What It's Worth*
Written by Stephen Stills

First came the Gas Chambers.
Then came the Microwaves.
We will have our Nuremberg too.

How does the oppressor best you?
How do they subdue?

3

Besides their cruelty and violence, what ends do they pursue?

It has rarely been stated explicitly.
We think that it goes without saying.
But it must be stated.

They kill us quietly, silently, and invisibly.
They make a game of it.

They divide us, turn us against one another, and turn our ideas against us.

That is how they kill us.
That is what they do.

Our identity, self-determination, and sovereignty are the very elements under attack, to say nothing of our right to life, liberty, and the pursuit of happiness, or our right to be let alone.

And we have still not developed an adequate response to their strategy.

We have never shied from battle. Indeed, on the battlefield itself we are often victorious. But elsewhere, we are continuously and unceremoniously bested.

We can no longer afford this. Nor can we afford diplomacy or goodwill when it comes to the oppressor.

We must act proactively and not reactively to predict
and anticipate their crimes against us.

To do so, we must see the battlefield as it exists not in our minds, but in reality.

War is no longer war.
War has become the war crime.

We are no longer in the realm of war, we are now firmly in the realm of war crimes. Hence our current malaise.

We are made to suffer the crimes of our oppressor on a daily basis.

They enter our homes, our beds, our minds, and our dreams, leaving us exposed, deprived, damaged, and undone.

They are very literally killing us in our sleep.

19

Their weapons do a daily dance on our walls.
Their deadly frequencies whisper on our pillows.

Our beds are the new battlefield, our bodies and minds their playground.

We are targets of their every insidious intent.

They enter our utilities, our appliances, our infrastructure, our electronics without warning or cause and justify their actions with what they leave behind.

They are terrorists who turn the frown of suspicion upon us, assaulting our every waking hour, our every step.

24

We sit defenseless against them and stand hopeless in
every direction.

25

They infiltrate our every effort and frustrate our every
end.

They paint us as enemies of the people, playing our battlecries negatively in their eardrums, as "evidence" that we are to be avoided.

27

They propagate every lie and false report they can think of in an effort to undermine and unsettle us.

They delight in keeping us on the move.

29

They are a vicious and ungodly enemy indeed.

What they call urban warfare and crowd control we know as unconstitutionality...the beginning of the end.

We suffer their injustices day in and day out without recourse to the law, the legislature, or the courts.

32

We are, in fact, prisoners in our own bodies.
By the time we realize it, we are already in shackles.

This is what it means to move from the realm of war into the realm of the war crime.

This is what it means to be a modern slave.

Who is our advocate?
Where is our Nuremberg?

How do we unseat this occupier?
How do we defeat this oppressor?

37

We must turn now to the lessons of Che Guevara and the Cuban Revolution.

Let us not forget that the principal reason to conduct guerrilla warfare within a country is because all peaceful and legal means of recourse have been exhausted.

As Guevara tells us, the "three fundamental lessons" of the Cuban Revolution are:

1) Popular forces can win a war against the army.

2) It is not necessary to wait until all conditions for making revolution exist; the insurrection can create them.

3) In underdeveloped America, the countryside is the basic area for armed fighting.

Tactics include hit-and-run strikes, protracted combat at a distance, and sabotage.

Finally, let us not forget that the guerrilla is not merely a soldier, but a dedicated social reformer who fights for a cause, "a disciplined ascetic."

42

The guerrilla should set an example which will inspire followers and forge solidarity with the people.

43

"The [people] must always be helped technically, economically, morally, and culturally." To this end, "the guerrilla fighter must be a sort of guiding angel."

Lastly, our tactics must be adapted to local circumstances.

We have already begun to:

1) Liberate the hospitals
2) Activate the libraries
3) Empower the students

46

It is time now for the Old Guard to carry us to the training grounds, arm and supply us, provide for our loved ones, and deliver us into action.

Let this be our benediction.

48

Amen.

# ABOUT THE AUTHOR

Champion Muthle aka Daniel Maree is an award-winning Writer-Director, Creative and Cultural Strategist, Independent Journalist, Inventor, Philosopher, Creative Technologist, Afro-Futurist, and Social Entrepreneur. He is a Frederick Douglass Scholar and Forbes 30 Under 30 Honoree for Social Entrepreneurship. His work has been featured in the MoMA and the Library of Congress.

www.ingramcontent.com/pod-product-compliance
Lightning Source LLC
Chambersburg PA
CBHW051416250726
48655CB00003B/1087